Everybody CRUMBLES My Cookie

Bill Rechin & Don Wilder

FAWCETT GOLD MEDAL • NEW YORK

A Fawcett Gold Medal Book
Published by Ballantine Books
Copyright © 1985, 1983 by News Group Chicago, Inc.

Library of Congress Catalog Card Number: 84-90958

ISBN 0-449-12644-7

Printed in Canada

First Edition: February 1985

10 9 8 7 6 5 4 3 2 1

KA PL OP

IT'S TOUGH TO GET OLD.

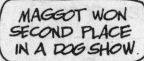

CRASH

YOU'VE BEEN DEPRESSED FOR DAYS.... WHAT'S WORRYING YOU?

I JUST REALIZED.... I'M NOT EMBARRASSED BY PROBLEM DANDRUFF.

WHY DIDN'T YOU HIT BACK AT ME?

I BELIEVE IN TURNING THE OTHER KNEECAP.

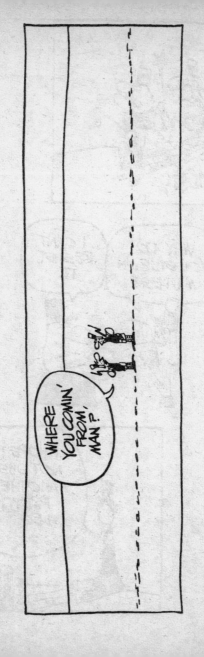